THE JOKE BATTLE

Dick v Dom

THE JOKE BATTLE

MACMILLAN CHILDREN'S BOOKS

First published 2018 by Macmillan Children's Books
an imprint of Pan Macmillan
20 New Wharf Road, London N1 9RR
Associated companies throughout the world
www.panmacmillan.com

ISBN 978-1-5098-8926-6

Text and illustrations copyright © McCourt Out Media and Dark Wood Productions 2018
Illustrated by Dave Chapman

The right of McCourt Out Media and Dark Wood Productions to be identified
as the authors of this work has been asserted by them in
accordance with the Copyright, Designs and Patents Act 1988.

1 3 5 7 9 8 6 4 2

A CIP catalogue record for this book is available from
the British Library.

Designed by The Dimpse
Printed and bound by CPI Group (UK) Ltd, Croydon CR0 4YY

CONTENTS

INTRODUCTION

Welcome to the ultimate JOKE fight, the ultimate JOKE showdown – it's Dick v Dom's JOKE battle! In this book you will find some of the funniest and unfunniest jokes known to humankind, but who will be funnier – Dick or Dom? You decide. On each page you'll find a score sheet to tick to show whose joke you thought was better.

Will it make you do naff-all, a little titter, gurgle like a fat baby, spit like a whale's blow-hole or laugh until you trump?

Are you ready?

It's fight time!

DICK   DOM

ANIMALS

There are around 7 billion humans roaming the earth compared to a million trillion ants – which means they could carry your granny up the stairs in forty-five seconds! Dick's favourite animal is a walrus as he comes from a long line of walruses and Dom's favourite is a horse as their rubbery lips look like they could rub out the Oxford English Dictionary.

What's the worst thing about being an octopus?

Washing your hands before dinner!

I'M PROTESTING ABOUT THE OCTOPUS JOKE ON THIS PAGE. I HAVE TENTACLES, NOT HANDS. OK?

OCTO-PROTEST

What's the best way to catch a fish?

Ask someone to throw it at you.

WHO'S FUNNIEST?

DICK DOM

1. Naff all

2. A little titter

3. Gurgling like a fat baby

4. Spitting like a whale's blow-hole

5. Laughed until I trumped!

THIS IS AN OCTOPUS WITH HANDS. RIDICULOUS. HAPPY NOW?

What did the tuna family say when a submarine went by?

'Oh, look, a tin full of people!'

What do you call a fish without an eye?

A fsh.

DICK DOM SCORE!

1.
2.
3.
4.
5.

What do whales eat?

Fish and ships.

DICK v DOM

What do you call a grasshopper with no legs?

A grasshover.

SCORE!

	DICK	DOM
1.		
2.		
3.		
4.		
5.		

Why do skunks argue a lot?
Because they like to raise a stink.

What medicine do you
give a sick horse?
Cough stirrup.

DICK   DOM   SCORE!

1.
2.
3.
4.
5.

5

What do farmers talk about when milking cows?

Udder nonsense.

What do you call a lazy baby kangaroo?

A pouch potato.

DICK DOM **SCORE!**

1.

2.

3.

4.

5.

What's invisible and smells like carrots?

Bunny farts.

ROTTEN CARROT STINK

What do you call a pile of kittens?

A meow-ntain.

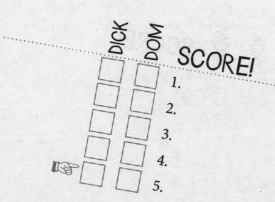

DICK DOM

SCORE!

1.
2.
3.
4.
5.

7

What goes 'OOOOO!'?
A cow with no lips.

How do you move a
really heavy pig?
Use a pork-lift truck.

SCORE!

DICK DOM

1.
2.
3.
4.
5.

What should you do if
a dog eats your pencil?

Use a pen instead.

What was on special
offer at the pet shop?

'Buy one dog, get one flea.'

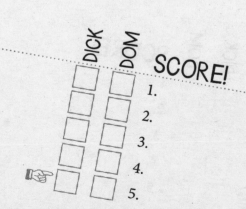

DICK DOM

SCORE!

1.

2.

3.

4.

5.

9

What do you get if you cross a skunk with a bat?

A nasty smell that hangs around all day.

What sound do hedgehogs make when they kiss?

'Ouch!'

SCORE!

	DICK	DOM
1.		
2.		
3.		
4.		
5.		

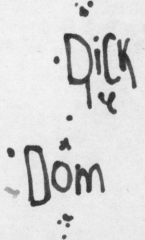

DICK

DOM

What do you call
someone with an
elephant on his head?

Squashed.

What kind of gum
do bees chew?

Bumble gum.

DICK DOM SCORE!

1.
2.
3.
4.
5.

DICK
DOM

TOTAL ANIMALS

11

2 SCHOOL

WARNING! This next introduction contains no lies.

School is great. We loved school. You love school. School will be the happiest time of your life. Teachers are great. School dinners are delicious. School is better than being on holiday.
WARNING! The first warning was a lie.

DICK AND DOM'S
SCHOOL FOR
EVERYONE

ALWAYS OPEN!
AMAZING SCHOOL!
(CLOSED WEDNESDAYS)
AND SUNDAY → TUESDAY
ENDLESS FUN!
(SHUT ON THURSDAY)
AND FRIDAY MORNING.
ONLY £10.00 A DAY.
IT'S NOT A PORTALOO
DRESSED UP AS A
SCHOOL.
(WE DIDN'T MAKE THE
CARDBOARD BITS.)

Teacher: Dom, can you find New Zealand on the map, please?

Dom: There it is, sir.

Teacher: Now, Dick, who discovered New Zealand?

Dick: Dom did.

Teacher: You missed school yesterday, didn't you, Dom?

Dom: Not even slightly.

WHO'S FUNNIEST?

DICK DOM

1. Naff all
2. A little titter
3. Gurgling like a fat baby
4. Spitting like a whale's blow-hole
5. Laughed until I trumped!

Teacher: Dick, I hope I didn't see you looking at Dom's paper.

Dick: *I hope you didn't either.*

Teacher: What came after the Stone Age and the Bronze Age?

Dom: *The Saus age?*

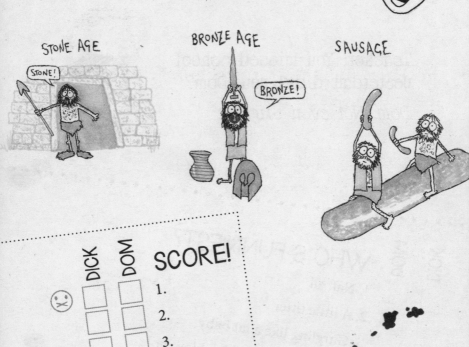

STONE AGE

STONE!

BRONZE AGE

BRONZE!

SAUSAGE

DICK DOM SCORE!

1.
2.
3.
4.
5.

14

Teacher: If you had five chocolate bars, and your little brother asked you for one, how many would you have left?

Dick: Five.

Teacher: What did your parents say about your report card?

Dom: Shall I leave out the bad language?

Teacher: Of course.

Dom: OK, then they didn't say anything.

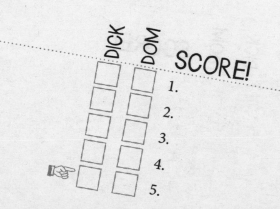

DICK DOM SCORE!

1.
2.
3.
4.
5.

What do you do if a teacher rolls her eyes at you?

Pick them up and roll them back to her.

Why did the new boy steal a chair from the classroom?

Because the teacher told him to take a seat.

SCORE!

	DICK	DOM
1.		
2.		
3.		
4.		
5.		

Teacher: Why is your homework in your father's handwriting?

Dick: I used his pen.

Teacher: Could you please pay a little attention?

Dom: I'm paying as little attention as I can.

DICK
v
Dom

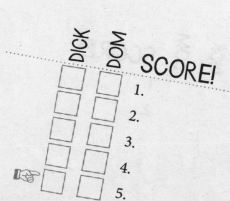

DICK DOM SCORE!

1.

2.

3.

4.

5.

Teacher: Name two days of the week that start with 't'.

Dick: Today and Tomorrow.

Teacher: What nationality are you?

Dom: Well, my father was born in Iceland and my mother was born in Cuba. So I reckon that makes me an ice cube.

	DICK	DOM	SCORE!
☹	☐	☐	1.
	☐	☐	2.
	☐	☐	3.
	☐	☐	4.
☺	☐	☐	5.

DICK

Our teacher's an ancient treasure.
We often wonder who dug her up.

Teacher: What do we do
with crude oil?
Dom: *Teach it some manners.*

Teacher: If I had 15 marbles in my right trouser pocket, 25 marbles in my left trouser pocket, 20 marbles in my right hip pocket and 30 marbles in my left hip pocket, what would I have?

Dick: Heavy trousers, sir.

Teacher: Are you going to visit Egypt?

Dom: I sphinx so.

SCORE!

	DICK	DOM	
☓	☐	☐	1.
	☐	☐	2.
	☐	☐	3.
	☐	☐	4.
☺	☐	☐	5.

Teacher: What can you tell me about Queen Victoria?

Dick: She's dead.

Dom: I think my English teacher loves me.

Dick: Why?

Dom: She keeps putting little kisses all over my homework just like these: X X X X!

SCORE!

DICK DOM

1.
2.
3.
4.
5.

21

Teacher! Teacher! I don't want to go to France.

Shut up and keep swimming!

What do maths teachers eat at Halloween?

Pumpkin pi.

SCHOOL TOTAL

DICK

DOM

DICK DOM

SCORE!

1.
2.
3.
4.
5.

3 FOOD

CHIPS!

Chips with salt,
Chips and gravy,
Chips with lumpy custard, maybe?
Chips in dips,
Chips with chips,
Chips that make you lick your lips.
Fish 'n' chips,
Chips 'n' fish,
Chips can go with every dish.
Chips 'n' sausage,
Chips 'n' pie,
If chips run out, I'll start to cry.

23

Waiter! Waiter! Will my pizza be long?

Waiter: No, sir, it will be round.

How did the butcher introduce his wife?

Meat patty.

WHO'S FUNNIEST?

DICK DOM

1. Naff all

2. A little titter

3. Gurgling like a fat baby

4. Spitting like a whale's blow-hole

5. Laughed until I trumped!

Have you heard the butter joke?

Don't spread it!

Waiter! Waiter! Do you serve crabs here?

Waiter: Yes, sir. We'll serve just about anybody.

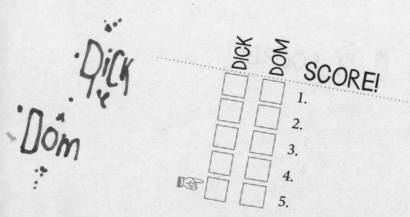

DICK   DOM   SCORE!

1.
2.
3.
4.
5.

Dick
Dom

How do you drain your Christmas Brussels' sprouts?

With an advent colander.

Orange
Juice
Concentrate

Why did the man stare at the can of orange juice?

Because it said 'concentrate'.

SCORE!

DICK DOM

1.
2.
3.
4.
5.

How does Good King Wenceslas like his pizza?

Deep-pan, crisp and even.

Who hides in the bakery at Christmas?

A mince spy.

I GO NOW BEFORE HE EATS MY HEAD.

DICK DOM

SCORE!

1.

2.

3.

4.

5.

What did the cannibal order for takeaway?

Pizza with everyone on it.

THIS PIZZA IS JUST TOO BIG.

DICK AND DOMINO'S PIZZA

What's a snowman's favourite Mexican food?

Brurrr-itos.

SCORE!

DICK DOM

1.
2.
3.
4.
5.

Why did Santa tell off one of his elves?

Because he was goblin his Christmas dinner.

How does the man in the moon eat his food?

In satellite dishes.

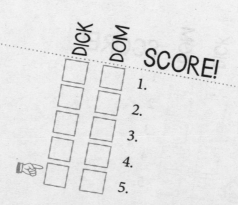

DICK DOM SCORE!

1.
2.
3.
4.
5.

What do cats call mice on skateboards?

Meals on Wheels.

DICK -e DOM

How can you tell if an elephant has been in your refrigerator?

Footprints in the butter.

	DICK	DOM	SCORE!
😖	☐	☐	1.
	☐	☐	2.
	☐	☐	3.
	☐	☐	4.
😊	☐	☐	5.

What is Dracula's
favourite fruit?

A blood orange.

Why did the mushroom
tell jokes?

Because he's a fungi.

HEY! I'M
A FUN GUY.

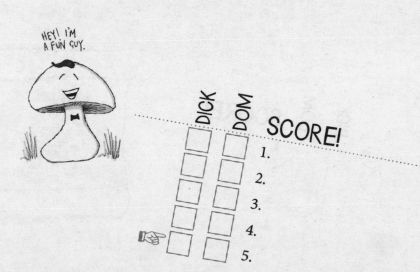

DICK   DOM   SCORE!

1.

2.

3.

4.

5.

Why was the bread sad?

Because it wanted to be kneaded by someone.

Why did the tomato blush?

Because it saw the salad dressing.

SCORE!

DICK   DOM

1.
2.
3.
4.
5.

DICK
V
DOM

What nut always has a cold?

The cashew.

What is a pretzel's favourite dance?

The twist.

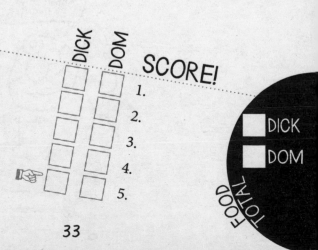

DICK DOM

SCORE!

1.
2.
3.
4.
5.

DICK
DOM

FOOD TOTAL

33

DOCTOR, DOCTOR

Dom's doctor was called Dr Biggin. In his spare time he was a magician.

One day he went to take out his appendix but instead pulled out a white rabbit called Boris with a crooked ear. Dick's doctor was called Dr Moffatt, a part-time plumber. He gave him a heart transplant, but instead of a new heart he replaced it with a cauliflower.

Doctor, Doctor, I feel like a racehorse.

Doctor: Take one of these every four laps!

Doctor, Doctor, I've broken my arm in two places.

Doctor: Well, don't go back to those places, then.

WHO'S FUNNIEST?

DICK DOM

1. Naff all
2. A little titter
3. Gurgling like a fat baby
4. Spitting like a whale's blow-hole
5. Laughed until I trumped!

 Doctor, Doctor, I've got so much wind. Do you have anything for it?

Doctor: Yes, here's a kite. Now go fly it!

Doctor, Doctor, I've swallowed a clock!

Doctor: There's no cause for alarm.

Patient: Doctor, Doctor, I couldn't drink my medicine after my bath like you told me to.

Doctor: Why not?

Patient: Well, after I'd drunk the bath, I didn't have room for the medicine!

Doctor, Doctor, can I get a second opinion?

Doctor: Absolutely – come back again tomorrow.

DICK DOM SCORE!
1.
2.
3.
4.
5.

37

DiCK

Doctor, Doctor, I've swallowed a dictionary!

Doctor: Shh! Don't breathe a word to anybody.

QOM

Doctor, Doctor I feel like a pack of cards.

Doctor: I'll deal with you later.

DICK DOM SCORE!

1.
2.
3.
4.
5.

38

Doctor, Doctor, I feel like a piano.

Doctor: Sit down while I make some notes.

Doctor, Doctor my little boy has just swallowed a roll of film.

Doctor: Well, let's just wait and see if anything develops.

DICK   DOM

SCORE!

1.
2.
3.
4.
5.

Doctor, Doctor, I think I'm suffering from déjà vu.

Doctor: Didn't I see you yesterday?

Doctor, Doctor, I feel like an apple.

Doctor: We must get to the core of this.

DICK DOM SCORE!

1.

2.

3.

4.

5.

DICK

DOM

Doctor, Doctor, you've taken out my tonsils, my adenoids, my gall bladder, my varicose veins and my appendix, but I still don't feel well.

Doctor: That's quite enough out of you.

Doctor: You seem to be in excellent health. Your pulse is as regular as clockwork.

Patient: That's because you've got your hand on my watch.

DICK   DOM   SCORE!
1.
2.
3.
4.
5.

Doctor, Doctor, everyone thinks I'm a liar.

Doctor: I can't believe that.

Patient: Doctor, Doctor, my sister thinks she is a lift.

Doctor: Well, tell her to come up.

Patient: I can't – she doesn't stop at this floor.

THIS IS MY SISTER. SHE DOESN'T THINK SHE'S A LIFT, SHE ACTUALLY IS A LIFT.

Yeah, I'm a lift. Hi.

SCORE!

	DICK	DOM
☹	☐	☐	1.
	☐	☐	2.
	☐	☐	3.
	☐	☐	4.
☺	☐	☐	5.

Doctor: You need new glasses.

Patient: But I haven't told you what's wrong with me yet.

Doctor: I could tell as soon as you walked in through the window.

Doctor, Doctor, I keep thinking I'm a bee.

Doctor: Buzz off. Can't you see I'm busy?

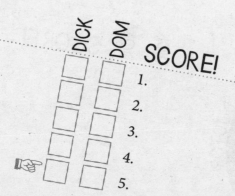

Doctor, Doctor, I keep thinking there are two of me.

Doctor: One at a time, please.

Doctor, Doctor, I keep thinking I'm a spider.

Doctor: What a web of lies.

DOCTOR, DOCTOR
TOTAL

☐ DICK
☐ DOM

DICK DOM SCORE!

1.
2.
3.
4.
5.

44

5 KNOCK, KNOCK

The knock, knock joke was invented by Mr Knocker and Mrs Knocker in 1856.

The Knockers thought they were funny but, in fact, people all over town used to think they were silly knockers. The Knockers knocked on people's knockers and when they answered the door they would tell knock, knock jokes. Everyone found this funny apart from the Ding-Dong family. They tried to invent the ding-dong joke but it failed because the door bell hadn't been invented yet. Thus the knockers came to power and the knock, knock joke was born.

Knock, knock.

Who's there?

Bella.

Bella who?

Bella not working – that's why I knocka.

Knock, knock.

Who's there?

King Tut.

King Tut who?

King Tut-key fried chicken!

KING TUT-KEY FRIED CHICKEN

DICK   DOM

WHO'S FUNNIEST?

1. Naff all
2. A little titter
3. Gurgling like a fat baby
4. Spitting like a whale's blow-hole
5. Laughed until I trumped!

46

Knock, knock.
Who's there?
Honeycomb.
Honeycomb who?
Honeycomb your hair!

Knock, knock.
Who's there?
Luke.
Luke who?
Luke through the spyhole
and you'll find out!

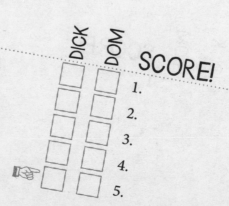

DICK DOM

SCORE!

1.
2.
3.
4.
5.

Knock, knock.

Who's there?

Cash.

Cash who?

No thanks, I'm allergic to nuts.

Knock, knock.

Who's there?

Archie.

Archie who?

Bless you!

DICK DOM SCORE!

1.
2.
3.
4.
5.

DICK & DOM

Knock, knock.
Who's there?
Howard.
Howard who?
Howard I know?

Knock, knock.
Who's there?
Armageddon.
Armageddon who?
Armageddon outta here!

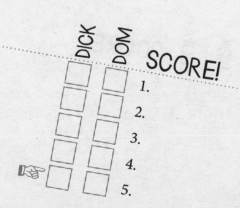

DICK	DOM	SCORE!
☐	☐	1.
☐	☐	2.
☐	☐	3.
☐	☐	4.
☐	☐	5.

Knock, knock.
Who's there?
Francis.
Francis who?
Francis a country in Europe.

Knock, knock.
Who's there?
Interrupting cow!
Interru—
Moo moooooo moo
mooooooooo moo!

SCORE!

DICK DOM

☒ 1.
   2.
   3.
   4.
☺ 5.

Knock, knock.

Who's there?

Nun.

Nun who?

Nun of your business!

Knock Knock!

Who's there?

Cowsgo.

Cowsgo who?

No they don't. Cowsgo moo.

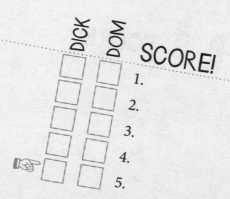

DICK DOM

SCORE!

1.

2.

3.

4.

5.

Knock, knock.

Who's there?

Lettuce.

Lettuce who?

Lettuce in! It's cold out here.

Knock, knock.

Who's there?

Dozen.

Dozen who?

Dozen anybody want to let me in?

SCORE!

	DICK	DOM
1.	☐	☐
2.	☐	☐
3.	☐	☐
4.	☐	☐
5.	☐	☐

Dick
v
Dom

Knock, knock.

Who's there?

Avenue!

Avenue who?

Avenue heard this joke before?

Knock, knock.

Who's there?

Little old lady?

Little old lady who?

Wow! I didn't know you could yodel.

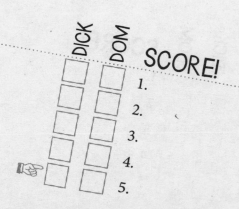

DICK   DOM   SCORE!

1.
2.
3.
4.
5.

53

Knock, knock.
Who's there?
Figs.
Figs who?
Figs the doorbell – it's broken!

Knock, knock.
Who's there?
Tank.
Tank who?
You're welcome!

DICK   DOM   SCORE!

1.
2.
3.
4.
5.

Knock, knock.

Who's there?

Dewey.

Dewey who?

Dewey have to keep telling silly jokes?

Knock, knock.

Who's there?

Snow.

Snow who?

Snowbody!

SCORE!

DICK DOM

1.
2.
3.
4.
5.

KNOCK, KNOCK TOTAL

DICK
DOM

55

 # SPORT

Did you know that the first footballs were made out of pig bladders (that's the bit that holds the pig's wee before it has a big pig wee).

Cricket bats were made out of left over stale sandwiches from rubbish weddings. The first snooker table used to be a swimming pool but the balls sank. The first golf clubs were stiff upside-down flamingos with hard hats.

DICK
v
Dom

What do you do if you're too hot at a football match?

Sit next to a fan.

Dick: My doctor says I can't play football.

Dom: Oh, so he's seen you play too, has he?

WHO'S FUNNIEST?

DICK DOM

1. Naff all
2. A little titter
3. Gurgling like a fat baby
4. Spitting like a whale's blow-hole
5. Laughed until I trumped!

Dick's dad: Why don't you go and play football with Dom?

Dick: I'm tired of kicking him around.

What is a ghost's favourite position in soccer?

Ghoul keeper.

SCORE!

	DICK	DOM
1.	☐	☐
2.	☐	☐
3.	☐	☐
4.	☐	☐
5.	☐	☐

Which football team should you not eat in a sandwich?

Oldham.

Where did the tennis players go on their date?

The tennis ball.

DICK DOM SCORE!

1.

2.

3.

4.

5.

Why did the footballer hold his boot to his ear?

Because he liked sole music.

What is a boxer's favourite drink?

Punch.

DICK
V
Dom

SCORE!

DICK DOM

1.
2.
3.
4.
5.

What do you get if you cross a skunk and a pair of tennis rackets?

Ping pong!

Why did the vampires cancel their rounders match?

Because they couldn't find their bats.

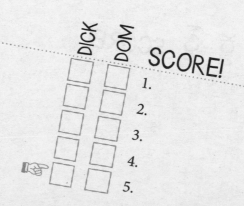

DICK DOM

SCORE!

1.
2.
3.
4.
5.

61

What stories are told by basketball players?

Tall stories!

Why was the ghost on the cheerleading squad?

It wanted to add a little team spirit.

SCORE!

DICK   DOM

1.

2.

3.

4.

5.

What does a footballer and a magician have in common?

Both do hat tricks!

What race is never run?

A swimming race.

DICK DOM

SCORE!

1.
2.
3.
4.
5.

What animal is the best cricket player?

The bat.

Why do footballers carry handkerchiefs?

Because they're always dribbling.

	DICK	DOM	SCORE!
🙁	☐	☐	1.
	☐	☐	2.
	☐	☐	3.
	☐	☐	4.
🙂	☐	☐	5.

Why can't Cinderella play football?

Because she's always running away from the ball.

Why did the golfer wear two pairs of pants?

In case he got a hole in one!

...I MIGHT GET A HOLE IN ONE...

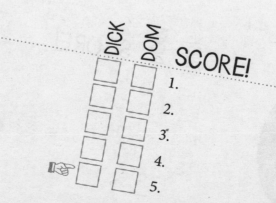

DICK DOM SCORE!

1.
2.
3.
4.
5.

Why did the man keep doing the backstroke?

Because he'd just eaten and didn't want to swim on a full stomach!

Today a man knocked on my door and asked for a small donation towards the local swimming pool. I gave him a glass of water.

SPORT TOTAL

☐ DICK
☐ DOM

DICK DOM SCORE!

1.
2.
3.
4.
5.

GEOGRAPHY

We didn't do Geography at school so we don't know where we are right now.

Do you know where you are right now? Does anybody know where they are right now? Where are we, who are we and most importantly what are we? Oh no, this is getting deep. I think our brains are about to explode!

AN IN-DEPTH MAP OF THE WORLD

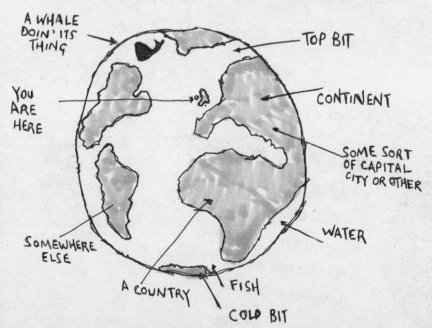

A WHALE DOIN' ITS THING

TOP BIT

YOU ARE HERE

CONTINENT

SOME SORT OF CAPITAL CITY OR OTHER

SOMEWHERE ELSE

WATER

A COUNTRY

FISH

COLD BIT

What do you call the small rivers that run into the Nile?

Juveniles.

What is the capital of England?

E.

WHO'S FUNNIEST?

DICK DOM

1. Naff all
2. A little titter
3. Gurgling like a fat baby
4. Spitting like a whale's blow-hole
5. Laughed until I trumped!

How do we know that Earth won't come to an end?

Because it's round.

MISS WORLD

What is the fastest country in the world?

Russia.

	DICK	DOM	SCORE!
1.	☐	☐	
2.	☐	☐	
3.	☐	☐	
4.	☐	☐	
5.	☐	☐	

DICK

DOM

In which city can you just wander around aimlessly?

Rome.

In which country are you most likely to slip and fall?

Greece.

DICK DOM **SCORE!**

☹

1.
2.
3.
4.
5.

☺

70

How do you find out
what the weather's
like at the top of a
mountain?

Climate.

Where did the bad
choir go on holiday?

Singapore.

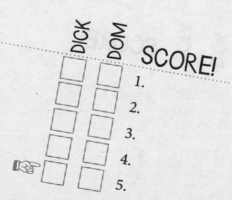

DICK DOM

SCORE!

1.

2.

3.

4.

5.

What is smarter, longitude or latitude?

Longitude, because it has 360 degrees.

What always sits in the corner but can move all round the world?

A stamp.

SAM-WO-WO

SPRAT

ISLE DU BOIS

McCOURTSKILL ISLAND

PLOOPY

PORK

MORNING, CLASS. TODAY I'VE INVENTED SOME COUNTRIES – JUST TO CONFUSE YOU. LEARN THEM ALL IN TEN SECONDS.

CHER

THE LAND OF POCKETS

LES

SLOBBADOBBA

FABWAMP

TWAPCAPS

BLAART PHWOOARY

REPUBLIC OF TOMMY

PAMELADOOVE

DICK	DOM	SCORE!
☺		1.
	2.
	3.
	4.
☺		5.

What has four eyes but can't see?

Mississippi.

In which country is the fastest growing capital city?

Ireland – it's Dublin every year.

DICK   DOM   SCORE!

1.

2.

3.

4.

5.

Why is it easy to get into Florida?

Because there are so many keys.

Geography teacher: Where is Timbuktu?

Dom: Between Timbukone and Timbukthree.

SCORE!

	DICK	DOM	
☹	☐	☐	1.
	☐	☐	2.
	☐	☐	3.
	☐	☐	4.
☺	☐	☐	5.

What is in the
middle of the sea?

The letter 'e'.

What is round at the ends
and high in the middle?

Ohio.

DICK DOM SCORE!

1.
2.
3.
4.
5.

What is the
spiciest country?

Chile.

TONIGHT ON THE
ENGLISH CHANNEL:
THE QUEEN IN A CUP
OF TEA WITH A UNION
JACK AND DAME JUDI
DENCH.

Geography teacher:
Where is the English
Channel?

*Dom: I don't know – my
TV doesn't pick it up*

	DICK	DOM	SCORE!
😐			1.
			2.
			3.
			4.
😃			5.

Where is it always 90 degrees, but never hot?

The North and South Poles.

Which US state does the most laundry?

Washington!

Ooooh!

DICK   DOM   SCORE!

1.
2.
3.
4.
5.

DICK
DOM

GEOGRAPHY
TOTAL

SCIENCE

Did we like Science at school? DID WE LIKE SCIENCE AT SCHOOL? DID WE?!? HEY? DID WE . . . LOVE SCIENCE . . . AT SCHOOL?!?

Well, no, actually, we didn't. Because our school didn't have a Science lab, or a Science teacher, or Science lessons. Instead we just used to pour milk on Coco Pops and when the milk went brown we'd all freak out, screaming that we had 'created science'. Anyway . . . enjoy these science jokes you copper-sulphate crystal-hugging, Bunsen-burner lovers!!!

WEIRD SCIENCE!

FRANKINCENSE!

DRACLE A!

A SKELLINGTON!

CHUTNEY!

78

What did one magnet say
to the other magnet?

I find you very attractive.

Which travels faster:
heat or cold?

*Heat – you can catch
a cold.*

WHO'S FUNNIEST?

DICK DOM

1. Naff all
2. A little titter
3. Gurgling like a fat baby
4. Spitting like a whale's blow-hole
5. Laughed until I trumped!

How many theoretical physicists does it take to screw in a lightbulb?

Two. One to hold the bulb and the other to rotate the universe.

What did one earthquake say to the other earthquake?

It's not my fault.

DICK DOM SCORE!

1.
2.
3.
4.
5.

Where does bad
light end up?

In prism.

Why did the germ cross
the microscope?

To get to the other slide.

DICK DOM SCORE!

1.
2.
3.
4.
5.

81

What happens if you eat uranium?

You get atomic-ache.

What happens if you get a gigabyte?

It megahertz.

SCORE!

DICK DOM

1.
2.
3.
4.
5.

Dick: When I die I'm going to leave my brain to science.

Dom: Well, I suppose every little bit helps.

Why did the atom cross the road?

It was time to split.

DICK DOM SCORE!

1.

2.

3.

4.

5.

How much room is needed for fungi to grow?

As mushroom as possible.

Why are chemists great at solving problems?

They have all the solutions.

DICK DOM SCORE!

1.

2.

3.

4.

5.

I'm reading a great book on anti-gravity. I can't put it down.

What goes zzub zzub?

A bee flying backwards.

DICK DOM SCORE!

1.

2.

3.

4.

5.

Why can't you trust an atom?
They make up everything.

Do I know any
jokes about sodium?
Na.

SCORE!

	DICK	DOM	
😖	☐	☐	1.
	☐	☐	2.
	☐	☐	3.
	☐	☐	4.
😃	☐	☐	5.

I have many chemistry jokes. I'm just worried they won't get a good reaction.

I only tell science jokes 'periodically'.

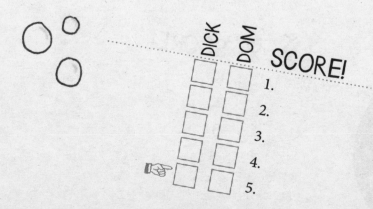

DICK   DOM   SCORE!

1.
2.
3.
4.
5.

Two blood cells fell in love . . .
but it was all in vein.

What did the proton
tell the electron?

Don't be so negative.

SCIENCE
TOTAL

DICK

DOM

DICK DOM SCORE!

1.
2.
3.
4.
5.

⑨ TRANSPORT

As we write this, we are on a train on the way to Shepton Mallet to visit Dick's Aunty Tina because she has one foot stuck in a pot of jam and the other foot stuck in the cat . . . flap!

We have to: get a train to Dorking, then a bus to Upton Snodsbury, get in a cab to North Piddle, fly to Nether Wallop, jump on a tram to Affpuddle and from there ride a tandem to Giggleswick. From there we turn left, right, left, then round the bend et voila: SHEPTON MALLET!

That was some journey, and now some transport jokes . . .

HOVER DONKEY

Dom: How could I ever leave you?

Dick: By bus, train, car, plane . . .

Ticket inspector: I'm sorry, sir, this train ticket is for London and this train's going to Oxford.

Dom: Oh dear! Does the driver know he's going the wrong way?

WHO'S FUNNIEST?

DICK DOM

☐ ☐ 1. Naff all

☐ ☐ 2. A little titter

☐ ☐ 3. Gurgling like a fat baby

☐ ☐ 4. Spitting like a whale's blow-hole

☐ ☐ 5. Laughed until I trumped!

Why are train drivers
anxious?

*Because their jobs are
always on the line.*

Why did the pilot
land his plane on top
of the house?

*Because the landing
lights were on.*

DICK & DOM

DICK DOM SCORE!

1.
2.
3.
4.
5.

Why are hairdressers such good drivers?

Because they know all the short cuts.

What do you call a vicar on a motorbike?

Rev.

SCORE!

	DICK	DOM
😖	1.	
	2.	
	3.	
	4.	
😊	5.	

What do monsters
make with cars?

Traffic jam.

Who earns a living by
driving his customers away?

A taxi driver.

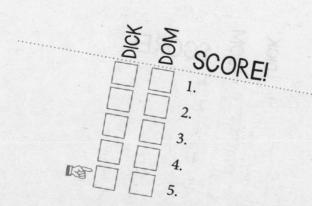

DICK DOM SCORE!

1.
2.
3.
4.
5.

93

What kind of ship
does Dracula have?

A blood vessel.

What do you call a train
loaded with toffee

A chew-chew train.

SCORE!

	DICK	DOM	
😣	☐	☐	1.
	☐	☐	2.
	☐	☐	3.
	☐	☐	4.
🙂	☐	☐	5.

What's the worst vegetable to serve on a boat?

Leeks.

What do you give a train conductor for his birthday?

Platform shoes.

DICK DOM

SCORE!

1.

2.

3.

4.

5.

What do you call a train that sneezes?

Achoo-achoo train.

Two goldfish are in a tank. One says to the other, 'Do you know how to drive this thing?'

SCORE!

	DICK	DOM	
☹	☐	☐	1.
	☐	☐	2.
	☐	☐	3.
	☐	☐	4.
☺	☐	☐	5.

What happens when a frog parks in a no-parking space?

It gets toad away.

What happened to the man that took the train home?

He had to give it back.

SCORE!

DICK DOM

1.
2.
3.
4.
5.

What did the boat say
to the pier?

What's up, doc.

Why did the opera singer
go sailing?

*Because she wanted to
hit the high Cs.*

What do you say to a
frog who needs a ride?

Hop in.

What do you get if
you cross a dog and
a plane?

A Jetsetter.

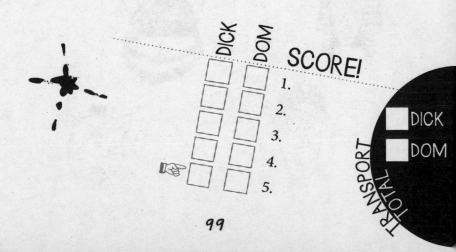

DICK · DOM · SCORE!

1.
2.
3.
4.
5.

DICK
DOM

TRANSPORT TOTAL

10 HISTORY

In the dictionary the meaning of 'history' is 'the study of past events'. So let's study our past events: we were born, we cried a lot, flicked beans up the wall, played with toy trains, learned how to crawl, had a bottle of milk before bed, splashed around in muddy puddles . . . AND THAT WAS ONLY LAST WEEK! So to celebrate all things in the past here are some old . . . I mean some historical and hysterical jokes!

Why did Henry VIII have so many wives?

He liked to chop and change.

Why is history fruity?

Because it's full of dates.

MMM. I LOVE ME SOME HISTORY.

WHO'S FUNNIEST?

DICK DOM

1. Naff all
2. A little titter
3. Gurgling like a fat baby
4. Spitting like a whale's blow-hole
5. Laughed until I trumped!

Which civilization
invented the fountain pen?

The Incas.

EGYPTIANS!

How do mummies begin
their emails?

Tomb it may concern.

SCORE!

DICK DOM

1.
2.
3.
4.
5.

Caesar: What's the
weather like?

Brutus: *Hail, Caesar.*

Dom: I wish I'd been alive a
few hundred years ago.

Teacher: Why?

Dom: There would have been
a lot less history to learn.

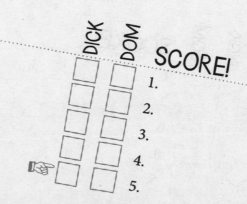

DICK DOM SCORE!

1.
2.
3.
4.
5.

Why did Robin Hood only rob the rich?

Because the poor didn't have anything worth stealing.

Why are mummies so good at keeping secrets?

Because they keep everything under wraps.

SCORE!

DICK   DOM

1.

2.

3.

4.

5.

What's purple and about 5,000 miles long?

The grape wall of China.

VIKINGS!

When a knight in armour was killed in battle, what sign did they put on his grave?

Rust in peace.

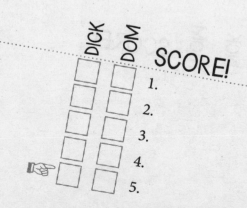

DICK DOM

SCORE!

1.
2.
3.
4.
5.

Why were the early days of history called the Dark Ages?

Because there were so many knights.

Teacher: Who can tell me where Hadrian's Wall is?

Dom: I expect it's round Hadrian's garden, miss.

	DICK	DOM	SCORE!
☹			1.
			2.
			3.
			4.
☺			5.

DICK

ROMANS!

Teacher: When was Rome built?

Dick: At night.

Teacher: Why did you say that?

Dick: Because my dad always says that Rome wasn't built in a day.

Why aren't you doing very well in History?

Because the teacher keeps asking about things that happened before I was born.

SCORE!

DICK	DOM	
☐	☐	1.
☐	☐	2.
☐	☐	3.
☐	☐	4.
☐	☐	5.

Who designed Noah's ark?
An ark-itect!

CAT PEOPLE!

What was the greatest
accomplishment of the
early Romans?

Speaking Latin!

DICK   DOM   SCORE!

☹ □ □ 1.
   □ □ 2.
   □ □ 3.
   □ □ 4.
☺ □ □ 5.

Dick
v
Dom

Why does history keep repeating itself?

Because we weren't listening the first time!

Who succeeded the first president of the USA?

The second one!

DICK DOM SCORE!

1.

2.

3.

4.

5.

How did Vikings communicate?

By Norse code!

Why couldn't cavemen send birthday cards?

The stamps wouldn't stick to the rocks.

GHOSTS AND MONSTERS

Once I decide to dress up as a ghost to scare Dom. So while he was out I put a sheet over my head, switched off the lights and stood in the corner waiting for him to come home.

Unfortunately I forgot that Dom had gone away for a two-week holiday to Blackpool. When he finally arrived home, I was still in the corner but slightly smelly and tired-looking. I looked a bit like this . . .

It didn't scare him! These ghostly jokes are SPOOOOOKTACULAR, though!

How do you make a witch itch?

Take away her 'w'.

What did one ghost say to the other ghost?

'Do you believe in people?'

WHO'S FUNNIEST?

DICK DOM

1. Naff all
2. A little titter
3. Gurgling like a fat baby
4. Spitting like a whale's blow-hole
5. Laughed until I trumped!

How do you join the
Dracula fan club?

*Send your name, address
and blood group.*

What do baby vampires
say at bedtime?

Read me a gory!

DICK DOM

SCORE!

1.

2.

3.

4.

5.

113

How did the Yeti feel
when he caught the flu?

Abominable.

First zombie: You
look tired.

*Second zombie: Yes,
I'm dead on my feet.*

SCORE!

DICK DOM

1.
2.
3.
4.
5.

First monster: Am I late for dinner?

Second monster: Yes. Everybody's been eaten.

How do monsters like their shepherd's pie?

Made with real shepherds.

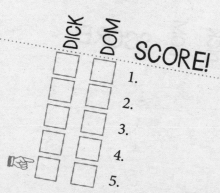

DICK   DOM   SCORE!

1.

2.

3.

4.

5.

115

What has a purple spotted body, ten hairy legs and big eyes on stalks?

I don't know, but there is one crawling up your leg!

How does a monster begin a fairy tale?

'Once upon a slime . . .'

What is the best way to speak to a monster?

From a long distance.

What monster plays the most April Fool's jokes?

Prankenstein.

DICK   DOM   SCORE!

1.

2.

3.

4.

5.

How do you stop a monster digging up your garden?

Take his spade away.

What happened when two huge monsters ran in a race?

One ran in short bursts, the other ran in burst shorts.

SCORE!

DICK DOM

1.
2.
3.
4.
5.

 How do you tell a good monster from a bad one?

If it's a good one, you will be able to talk about it later.

What did Frankenstein's monster say when he was struck by lightning?

Thanks, I needed that.

SCORE!

DICK DOM

1.
2.
3.
4.
5.

What happens if a big hairy monster sits in front of you at the movie theatre?

You miss most of the film.

What do you call a huge, ugly, slobbering, furry monster with cotton wool in his ears?

Anything you like – he can't hear you.

DICK DOM SCORE!

1.
2.
3.
4.
5.

How did the monster
cure his sore throat?

*He spent all day
gargoyling.*

What brings the monster's babies?

The Frankenstork.

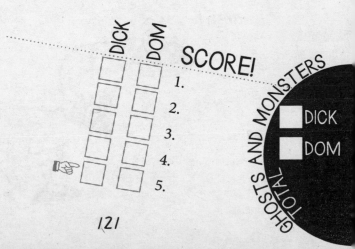

DICK

DOM

SCORE!

1.

2.

3.

4.

5.

GHOSTS AND MONSTERS

TOTAL

DICK

DOM

12 DINOSAURS

If we could be turned into dinosaurs, we would be called Dicklodocus and Domosaurus rex.

Our dinos would be stupid, with brains the size of peanuts (which is actually slightly bigger than our current brain sizes). We would only have two predator dinosaurs and they would be Teresaraptor may and the Corbinadon. Though scary to look at, their brains are actually the size of chickpeas. They wear party hats and spend their days blowing bubbles out of their ears and trying to eat soup with a fork. LUCKILY all these are extinct but these dino jokes definitely aren't.

Why do dinosaurs eat raw meat?

Because they can't cook.

What does a T rex eat?

Anything it wants.

WHO'S FUNNIEST?

DICK | DOM

1. Naff all
2. A little titter
3. Gurgling like a fat baby
4. Spitting like a whale's blow-hole
5. Laughed until I trumped!

What does a dinosaur get after exercise?

Dino-sore.

Why did the dinosaur cross the road?

Because the chicken hadn't evolved yet.

	DICK	DOM	SCORE!
☹	☐	☐	1.
	☐	☐	2.
	☐	☐	3.
	☐	☐	4.
☺	☐	☐	5.

What do you call a dinosaur that never quits?

Try-Try-Try-ceratops.

What followed the dinosaurs?

Their tails.

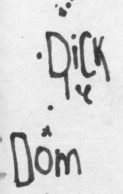

DICK DOM SCORE!

1.
2.
3.
4.
5.

How did dinosaurs
pass their exams?

With extinction.

Why are there old dinosaur
bones in the museum?

*Because they can't afford to
buy new ones.*

DICK   DOM   SCORE!

☹   1.

2.

3.

4.

☺   5.

Which is the scariest dinosaur?

The terrordactyl.

What makes more noise than a dinosaur?

Two dinosaurs.

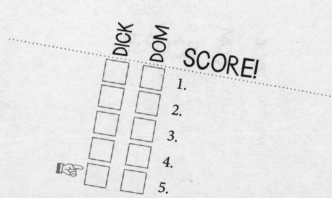

DICK DOM SCORE!

1.

2.

3.

4.

5.

What do you call a dinosaur that destroys everything?

Tyrannosaurus wrecks.

What do you call a dinosaur with an extensive vocabulary?

A thesaurus.

DICK DOM SCORE!

1.
2.
3.
4.
5.

What do you call a
dinosaur that won't
have a bath?

A stinkosaurus.

What would you get if
you crossed a dinosaur
with a pig?

Jurassic pork.

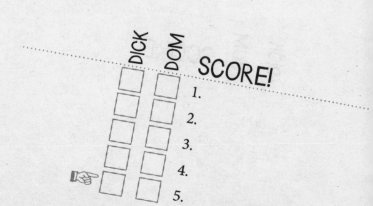

Why are dinosaurs no longer around?
Because they're eggs-stink.

What do you call a dinosaur
that eats fireworks?

Dino-mite.

JUST ONE MORE.
YUM-YUM...

FIREWORKS

FIREWOR

SCORE!

	DICK	DOM	
☹			1.
			2.
			3.
			4.
☺			5.

Why did the ankylosaurus catch the worm?

Because it was an early bird.

What do you get when a dinosaur sneezes?

Out of the way!

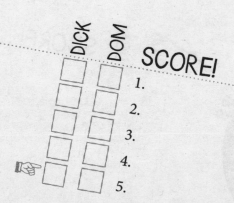

SCORE!

DICK DOM

1.
2.
3.
4.
5.

What do you say when you meet a two-headed dinosaur?

A: Hello, hello!

What does a triceratops sit on.

Its tricera-bottom.

DINOSAURS
TOTAL

☐ DICK
☐ DOM

DICK DOM SCORE!
☐ ☐ 1.
☐ ☐ 2.
☐ ☐ 3.
☐ ☐ 4.
☐ ☐ 5.

13 FAMILY

Some would say that your family is the most important thing in the world. Some would say that your family are the friends you can't choose. You're stuck with them . . . FOR LIFE! AND THAT'S THAT!

So:

Your grumpy Granny who spits in a tissue and wipes crumbs off your face. YOU'RE STUCK WITH HER.

Your older cousin who sits on your head and trumps just so he can get the remote control. YOU'RE STUCK WITH HIM.

Your Mum who says EVERY DAY without fail, 'How was school today'. YOU'RE STUCK WITH HER.

So what do you do? Simple . . . smear fish paste onto their door knobs while they are asleep so they stink of fish forever. (You're still stuck with them . . . but it'll make you laugh).

Dom: My nan was a medium.

Dixk: Really? Mine was an extra large.

DICK'S NAN

DOM'S NAN

Dom's dad: Who broke the window?

Dom: It was Dick, Dad. He ducked when I threw a stone at him.

WHO'S FUNNIEST?

DICK DOM

1. Naff all
2. A little titter
3. Gurgling like a fat baby
4. Spitting like a whale's blow-hole
5. Laughed until I trumped!

Dick's dad: Would you like any help with your homework?

Dick: No, thanks. I'd rather get it wrong on my own.

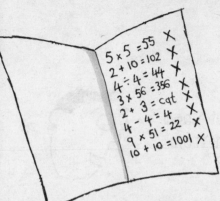

5 x 5 = 55 X
2 + 10 = 102 X
4 ÷ 4 = 44 X
3 x 56 = 356 X
2 + 3 = cat XX
4 - 4 = 4 XX
9 x 51 = 22 X
10 + 10 = 1001 X

Dom's sister: I can marry anyone I please.

Dom: But you don't please anyone.

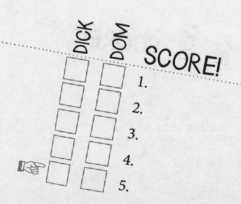

SCORE!

DICK DOM

1.
2.
3.
4.
5.

Why are Grandpa's teeth like the stars?

Because they come out at night.

Dom: Mum, you know that vase that's been handed down from generation to generation?

Dom's mum: Yes?

Dom: Well, this generation's dropped it.

SCORE!

DICK DOM

1.
2.
3.
4.
5.

Dick's dad: Didn't you hear me hammering on your bedroom door last night, Dick?

Dick: Don't worry, Dad. I was playing my music really loudly, so you didn't disturb me.

Dom: Mum, you know you're constantly worrying that I'll fail Maths?

Dom's mum: Yes?

Dom: Well, your worries are over.

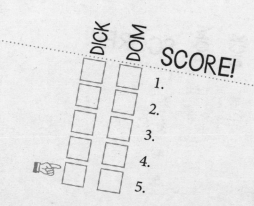

Dick's dad: I want to take my son out of this terrible Maths class.

Teacher: But he's top of the class.

Dick's dad: That's why I think it must be a terrible class.

MINI MUM

What do you call a small mother?

A minimum.

DICK   DOM   SCORE!

1.

2.

3.

4.

5.

138

What do young ghosts call their parents?

Deady and Mummy.

Dom: Dad, a monster's just bitten my foot off.

Dad: Well, keep out of the kitchen. I've just mopped the floor.

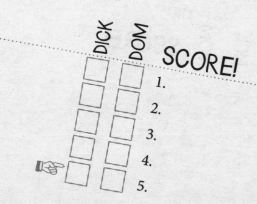

SCORE!

DICK	DOM	
☐	☐	1.
☐	☐	2.
☐	☐	3.
☐	☐	4.
☐	☐	5.

Dick: My sister's the school swot.

Dom: Does she do well in exams?

Dick: No, but she kills a lot of flies.

Dom: I won best costume at the Halloween party.

Dick: That's great.

Dom: Not really. I only went to pick up my little sister.

DICK   DOM   SCORE!

1.
2.
3.
4.
5.

Boy: My father's name is Laughing and my mother's name is Smiling.

Teacher: You must be kidding!

Boy: No, that's my brother. I'm Joking!

Dom: Where are the Himalayas?

Dom's dad: If you'd put things away, you'd know where to find them.

What time did Dad
go to the dentist?

Tooth hurty.

Father: Why did you get such a
low score in that exam?

Son: Absence!

Father: You were absent on the
day of the exam?

*Son: No, but the boy who sits
next to me was!*

Alfie was listening to his sister practise her singing. 'Sis,' he said, 'I wish you'd sing Christmas carols.'

'That's nice of you, Alfie,' she replied. 'Why?'

'Then I'd only have to hear you once a year!'

How do you know if your little brother is turning into a fridge?

See if a little light comes on whenever he opens his mouth!

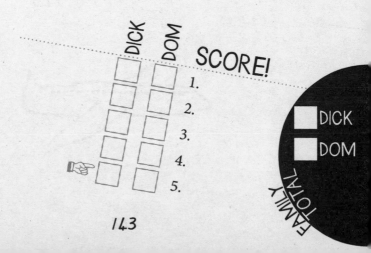

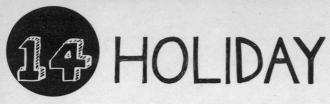

HOLIDAY

At school together we decided to start a new campaign to 'ban school forever and only have holidays'.

Unfortunately Dom wrote it the wrong way round and started a campaign to 'ban holidays forever and only have school'. This didn't go down so well with all the other kids in the school. So much so that they dressed him up as a large carrot and tried feeding him to the school rabbit! The rabbit took one bite and went green. Poor bunny! Luckily the bunny is alive and well, and helped us write these happy, hoppy holiday jokes.

What is brown, hairy and wears sunglasses?

A coconut on holiday.

Dick: What did you do in Austria?

Dom: *I thought about going skiing but then I let it slide.*

WHO'S FUNNIEST?

DICK DOM

1. Naff all
2. A little titter
3. Gurgling like a fat baby
4. Spitting like a whale's blow-hole
5. Laughed until I trumped!

Why did the crab blush?

Because the sea weed.

Dom: Hmmm. This room's OK, but I'd like one with a shower.

Hotel Owner: This isn't your room – it's the lift.

SCORE!

	DICK	DOM	
☹	☐	☐	1.
	☐	☐	2.
	☐	☐	3.
	☐	☐	4.
☺	☐	☐	5.

Dom: What was your hotel like?

Dick: Amazing. It had three swimming pools!

Dom: Three?

Dick: Yep – one full of hot water, one cold water and one empty.

Dom: What use was the empty pool?

Dick: It was for people who couldn't swim.

What did one rock pool say to the other?

Show us your mussels.

DICK DOM SCORE!

1.

2.

3.

4.

5.

147

Dom: How was your week skiing?

Dick: Interesting. I spent one day skiing and six in hospital.

Hotel guest: I'd like a room with a sea view, please.

Hotel receptionist: That's £40 extra per night.

Hotel guest: How much if I promise not to look?

SCORE!

	DICK	DOM	
☹	☐	☐	1.
	☐	☐	2.
	☐	☐	3.
	☐	☐	4.
☺	☐	☐	5.

How can you tell that elephants love to travel?

They always pack their own trunk.

What do you call six weeks of rain in Scotland?

Summer.

Dom: I just flew back from my holiday.

Dick: I bet your arms are tired.

Where do sheep go on holiday?

The Baaa-hamas!

The seaside resort we visited last summer was so boring that one day the tide went out and never came back.

Where do hamsters go on holiday?

Hamsterdam.

DICK   DOM

SCORE!

1.

2.

3.

4.

5.

What do you call a French
guy in sandals?

Phillipe Phloppe.

What do you call a dog on
the beach in the summer?

A hot dog.

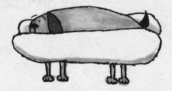

SCORE!

DICK	DOM	
☒ □	□	1.
□	□	2.
□	□	3.
□	□	4.
☺ □	□	5.

Where do pepperonis go on vacation?

The Leaning Tower of Pizza.

Why don't mummies go on holiday?

Because they are afraid to relax and unwind.

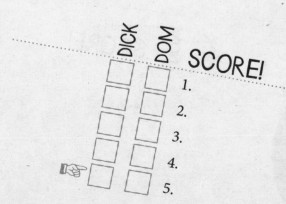

DICK DOM SCORE!

1.
2.
3.
4.
5.

Monica: Where did your mum go for her summer holiday?

Josh: Alaska.

Monica: Never mind. I'll ask her myself.

What did E.T.'s mother say to him when he got home?

'Where on Earth have you been?'

HOLIDAY TOTAL

DICK

DOM

DICK DOM SCORE!

1.
2.
3.
4.
5.

15 CHEESE

AND NOW, ladies and gentlemen,
inspired by cheese, here is a poem
about . . . CHEESE:*

Blue cheese, orange cheese, stinky cheese
and squeezy cheese.
Goats cheese, gooey cheese –
This one is whiffy cheese.
Cheese on crackers.
Cheese on toast;
Cheesy chips I love the most
With a pickled onion on a cocktail stick.
I'll eat cheese until I'm sick!

THE END

And now some truly cheeeesy jokes!

* This poem is in NO WAY similar to the chips poem from
earlier. It's TOTALLY DIFFERENT!

What did the mouse say when it broke its front teeth?

Hard cheese.

What cheese is made backwards?

Edam.

WHO'S FUNNIEST?

DICK

DOM

1. Naff all
2. A little titter
3. Gurgling like a fat baby
4. Spitting like a whale's blow-hole
5. Laughed until I trumped!

Why did the priest
like Swiss cheese?

*Because it was
hole-y.*

How do you handle
dangerous cheese?

Caerphilly.

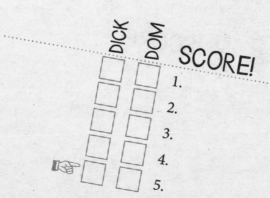

DICK DOM

SCORE!

1.
2.
3.
4.
5.

Did you hear about the cheesy comedian?

He had some crackers.

What do you call cheese that doesn't belong to you?

Nacho cheese.

DICK DOM SCORE!

1.
2.
3.
4.
5.

Why was the
cheesemonger
lopsided?

*He only had
one Stilton.*

Why is Christmas the
cheesiest holiday?

Because of baby cheese-us!

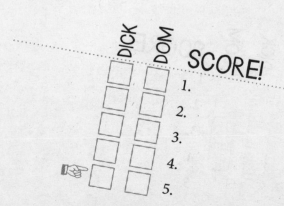

DICK DOM

SCORE!

1.

2.

3.

4.

5.

What's a pirate's
favourite cheese?

Chedd-AAR!

There was an explosion
at a cheese factory in
France. All that was
left was de Brie.

SCORE!

DICK DOM

1.
2.
3.
4.
5.

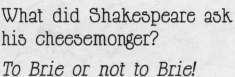

What did Shakespeare ask his cheesemonger?

To Brie or not to Brie!

What is a lion's favourite cheese?

Roar-quefort.

DICK DOM

SCORE!

1.

2.

3.

4.

5.

What do you call a monster made of cheese?

Gorgonzilla.

RAAAAAH

When can't you see a cheese?

When it's pasteurised.

SCORE!

DICK DOM

1.
2.
3.
4.
5.

What does cheese say
to itself in the mirror?

Halloumi.

What do you call
cheese that is sad?

Blue cheese.

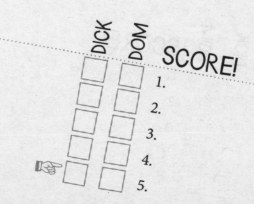

DICK DOM SCORE!

1.
2.
3.
4.
5.

163

How do you get a
mouse to smile?

Say cheese!

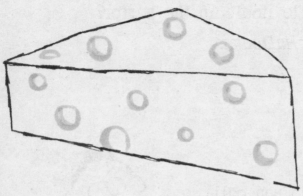

What do cheese salesmen say?

*That cheese may be Gouda, but
this one is Feta!*

	DICK	DOM	SCORE!
☹	☐	☐	1.
	☐	☐	2.
	☐	☐	3.
	☐	☐	4.
☺	☐	☐	5.

164

What cheese do you use to hide a small horse?

Marscapone.

Which genre of music appeals to most cheeses?

R'n'Brie.

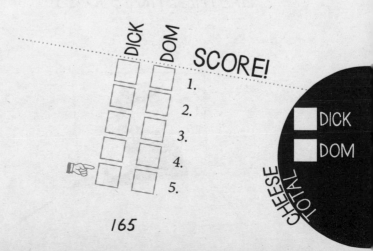

DICK

DOM

SCORE!

1.

2.

3.

4.

5.

DICK

DOM

CHEESE
TOTAL

 PIRATES

Our mate John decided that he wanted to be a pirate. He used to walk around the neighbourhood telling people to walk the plank.

Two problems:

We didn't live near the sea or a river, so people would have to fall off the plank and land 'SPLAT' on the floor.
He didn't have a plank, so problem number 1 never even happened.
John's mum also didn't let him buy a parrot so he walked around with a baked potato on his shoulder instead.
John was weird, but funny . . . JUST LIKE THESE PIRATE JOKES!

What's a pirate's favourite school subject?

Aaaart.

What do you get if you cross a pie and a rat?

A pirate.

WHO'S FUNNIEST?

DICK DOM

1. Naff all
2. A little titter
3. Gurgling like a fat baby
4. Spitting like a whale's blow-hole
5. Laughed until I trumped!

How much do pirates pay for their earrings?

A buccaneer.

Why does it take a pirate so long to learn the alphabet?

Because they can spend years at C.

	DICK	DOM	SCORE!
☹	☐	☐	1.
	☐	☐	2.
	☐	☐	3.
	☐	☐	4.
☺	☐	☐	5.

How much did the pirate pay for his peg leg and hook?

An arm and a leg.

How do ye turn a pirate furious?

Take away the 'p'.

DICK DOM SCORE!

1.
2.
3.
4.
5.

169

Why are pirates called pirates?

Because they aaaaarrrrr!

How do pirates communicate with each other?

With an Aye phone.

SCORE!

DICK DOM

1.
2.
3.
4.
5.

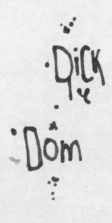

DICK

DOM

What's a pirate's favourite country?

Arrrrrrrrr-gentina.

How do pirates prefer to communicate?

Aye to aye!

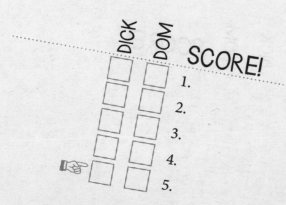

DICK DOM SCORE!

1.
2.
3.
4.
5.

How did the pirate get his ship so cheaply?

He bought it on sail.

Why did nobody want to play cards with the pirate?

Because he was standing on the deck.

SCORE!

	DICK	DOM	
☹	☐	☐	1.
	☐	☐	2.
	☐	☐	3.
	☐	☐	4.
☺	☐	☐	5.

172

What's orange and
sounds like a parrot?

A carrot.

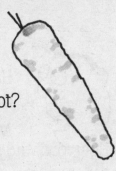

What does a pirate wear
for Halloween?

A pumpkin patch.

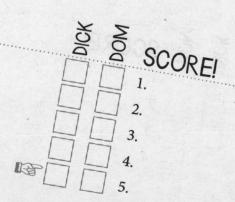

SCORE!

DICK DOM

1.
2.
3.
4.
5.

How did the pirate become
a boxing champion?

*Nobody could take on his
right hook.*

What's a pirate's favourite
star wars character?

Aaaaar2-D2.

SCORE!

DICK   DOM

1.
2.
3.
4.
5.

What are the ten letters of the pirate alphabet?

I, I, R and the seven Cs.

Where do pirates shop?

Aaaargos.

DICK   DOM   SCORE!

1.
2.
3.
4.
5.

175

Why are pirate flags always in a bad mood?

Because they have crossbones.

What did the pirate say when his wooden leg froze?

Shiver me timbers!

PIRATES TOTAL

DICK

DOM

SCORE!

DICK DOM

1.
2.
3.
4.
5.

17 SPACE

WARNING! If you read this, your head will open up and your brain will fly out of your head:

What is space?
How big is space?
Does space ever end?
Where does a black hole lead?
What is the sun?
Why is it even there?
Is there other life out there?
Where did I put my wallet?
What's for dinner tonight?
How many sheep could fit into a Mini?

Sorry . . .
got a
bit side-
tracked! Back to space
and some jokes that are
OUT OF THIS WORLD!!!

What's a spaceman's favourite game?

Astronauts and crosses.

What did Mars say to Saturn?

Give me a ring some time.

WHO'S FUNNIEST?

DICK DOM

☐ ☐ 1. Naff all

☐ ☐ 2. A little titter

☐ ☐ 3. Gurgling like a fat baby

☐ ☐ 4. Spitting like a whale's blow-hole

☐ ☐ 5. Laughed until I trumped!

What did the astronaut see in the frying pan?

An unidentified frying object.

Where do Martians go for a drink?

Mars bars.

DICK   DOM   SCORE!

1.

2.

3.

4.

5.

How do you get a
baby astronaut to sleep?

You rocket.

Where do aliens leave
their flying saucers?

At parking meteors.

DICK   DOM   SCORE!

1.

2.

3.

4.

5.

MERCURY

VENUS

YOU ARE HERE

EARTH

MARS

THE DEATH STAR

Why did the Martian go to the optician?

He had stars in his eyes.

What school do planets and stars go to study?

Univers-ity.

DICK

DOM

SCORE!

1.

2.

3.

4.

5.

JUPITER   SATURN   URANUS   NEPTUNE   PLUTO

Why did the cow go in the spaceship?

It wanted to see the moooooooon.

What do astronauts eat on?

Flying saucers.

SCORE!

	DICK	DOM	
😣	☐	☐	1.
	☐	☐	2.
	☐	☐	3.
	☐	☐	4.
😊	☐	☐	5.

What is an astronaut's favourite key on the keyboard?

The space bar.

What do you do when you see a spaceman?

Park in it, man.

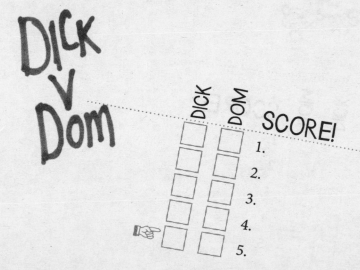

DICK
v
Dom

DICK   DOM   SCORE!

1.

2.

3.

4.

5.

What should you do when you see a green alien?

Wait until it's ripe.

What do you call an alien with three eyes?

An aliiien.

	DICK	DOM	SCORE!
😝	☐	☐	1.
	☐	☐	2.
	☐	☐	3.
	☐	☐	4.
😊	☐	☐	5.

How do you organize
a space party?

You planet.

Where do astronauts keep
their sandwiches?

In a launch box.

DICK

DOM

DICK DOM SCORE!

1.

2.

3.

4.

5.

185

What do you get if you cross Santa Claus with a space-ship?

A U-F-ho-ho-ho.

Why don't aliens eat clowns?

Because they taste funny.

SCORE!

DICK   DOM

1.

2.

3.

4.

5.

Why don't people like the restaurant on the moon?

Because there's no atmosphere.

What was the first animal in space?

The cow that jumped over the moon.

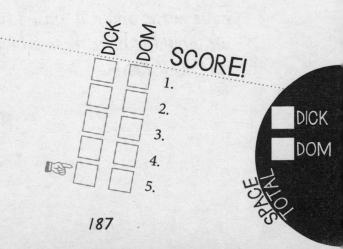

DICK   DOM

SCORE!

1.
2.
3.
4.
5.

DICK
DOM

SPACE TOTAL

18 MUSIC

Music was invented by a well-known caveman millions of years ago called Mandy.

He popped a straw up a dinosaur's nose and blew really hard and it made a funny squeaking noise. He called this B-flat minor! Mandy then worked out that if you did the same thing to eight dinosaurs of different sizes you would get eight different notes . . . and, THUS, THE FIRST BAND WAS BORN. Unfortunately the dinosaurs didn't like this and ate Mandy. Poor Mandy! BUT, if it wasn't for Mandy, we wouldn't have music and if it wasn't for music we wouldn't have these wonderful MUSIC JOKES!

What kind of music can you find in outer space?

Nep-tunes.

What do you get if you drop a piano down a mine shaft?

A-flat minor.

WHO'S FUNNIEST?

DICK DOM

1. Naff all
2. A little titter
3. Gurgling like a fat baby
4. Spitting like a whale's blow-hole
5. Laughed until I trumped!

Why did the orchestra have bad manners?

Because it didn't know how to conduct itself.

Why did the composer spend all his time in bed?

He wrote sheet music.

SCORE!

DICK DOM

1.
2.
3.
4.
5.

190

Why did the composer
climb the ladder?

To reach the high notes.

Which musical instrument can
be used to catch fish?

A castanet.

DICK DOM

SCORE!

1.
2.
3.
4.
5.

191

Why was the musician
arrested?

Because he got into treble.

Which composer
had the most colds?

Tchaikovsky.

SCORE!

DICK   DOM

1.

2.

3.

4.

5.

How do you wake up Lady Gaga?

Poker Face.

DiCK & DOM

What is the karate teacher's favourite composer?

Chopin!

DICK   DOM   SCORE!

1.

2.

3.

4.

5.

What's yellow,
weighs 1,000
pounds, and
sings?

*Two 500-pound
canaries!*

Why is a piano so
hard to open?

*Because the keys are
on the inside!*

DICK   DOM   SCORE!

☹ 1.
   2.
   3.
   4.
☺ 5.

What's the most
musical bone?

The trom-bone!

What makes music
on your hair?

A head band!

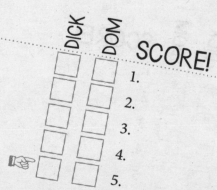

DICK DOM SCORE!

1.

2.

3.

4.

5.

How do you make a band stand?

Take their chairs away!

What do little penguins sing when their father brings fish home for dinner?

Freeze a Jolly Good Fellow!

SCORE!

	DICK	DOM
1.	☐	☐
2.	☐	☐
3.	☐	☐
4.	☐	☐
5.	☐	☐

What type of music are balloons scared of?

Pop music!

What's the most musical part of a turkey?

The drumstick!

DICK DOM SCORE!

1.
2.
3.
4.
5.

What's the most musical part of a fish?

The scales!

What's the difference between a piano and a fish?

You can tune a piano, but you can't tuna fish!

SCORE!

DICK DOM

1.
2.
3.
4.
5.

MUSIC TOTAL

DICK
DOM

Ha ha ha ha ha hardy ha ha ha ha hardy ha ha ha ha ha hardy ha . . . You are now probably rolling around the floor laughing. But who was funnier, Dick or Dom? It's time to tot up your scores and find out. Add up the points at the end of each section in the handy chart over the page, and – *voila* – you have a TOTAL.

THE WINNER IS

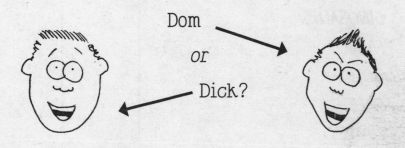

Dom or Dick?

SCORING

Who is the funniest?

	DICK	DOM
ANIMALS		
SCHOOL		
FOOD		
DOCTOR, DOCTOR		
KNOCK, KNOCK		
SPORT		
GEOGRAPHY		
SCIENCE		
TRANSPORT		
HISTORY		
GHOSTS		
DINOSAURS		
FAMILY		
HOLIDAY		
CHEESE		
PIRATES		
SPACE		
MUSIC		